# MEASURE UP MATH

# AREA

## Chris Woodford

**Gareth Stevens**
Publishing

Please visit our website, www.garethstevens.com. For a free color catalog of all our high-quality books, call toll-free 1-800-542-2595 or fax 1-877-542-2596.

**Library of Congress Cataloging-in-Publication Data**

Woodford, Chris.
Area / Chris Woodford.
    p. cm. — (Measure up math)
Includes index.
ISBN 978-1-4339-7434-2 (pbk.)
ISBN 978-1-4339-7435-9 (6-pack)
ISBN 978-1-4339-7433-5 (library binding)
1. Area measurement—Juvenile literature. I. Title.
QA465.W648 2013
516'.15—dc23

                                    2011045528


**Published in 2013 by**
Gareth Stevens Publishing
111 East 14th Street, Suite 349
New York, NY 10003

© 2013 Brown Bear Books Ltd

For Brown Bear Books Ltd:
Editorial Director: Lindsey Lowe
Managing Editor: Tim Harris
Children's Publisher: Anne O'Daly
Art Director: Jeni Child
Designer: Lynne Lennon
Picture Manager: Sophie Mortimer
Production Director: Alastair Gourlay

**Picture Credits:**
Key: t = top, tr = top right, b = bottom
**Front Cover: Shutterstock:** Leonid Meleca of Congress
**Interior: NASA:** 25, Earth Observatory 20, GSFC 13tr; **Shutterstock:** allensima 16, Marcel Clemens 26, Glenda M. Powers 23tr; Thinkstock: Hemera 8, 24br, istock 22, 27, Photos.com 12–13, 14–15.
All other artworks and photographs Brown Bear Books.
Brown Bear Books has made every attempt to contact the copyright holder. If anyone has any information could they please contact smortimer@windmillbooks.co.uk

All Artworks © Brown Bear Books Ltd

**Publisher's note to educators and parents:** Our editors have carefully reviewed the websites that appear on p. 31 to ensure that they are suitable for students. Many websites change frequently, however, and we cannot guarantee that a site's future contents will continue to meet our high standards of quality and educational value. Be advised that students should be closely supervised whenever they access the Internet.

Manufactured in the United States of America
1 2 3 4 5 6 7 8 9   12 11 10

CPSIA compliance information: Batch #BRS12GS: For further information contact Gareth Stevens, New York, New York at 1-800-542-2595.

# CONTENTS

# WHAT IS AREA?

length

height

**length x height = area**

►►► **S**uppose you wanted to paint the walls of your room. You could figure out how many cans of paint to buy if you knew how big the walls are. The size of a flat surface, such as a wall, is called its area. A big wall has a larger area than a small wall.

▲ **The height of a wall is the distance from the floor to the ceiling. The length of a wall is the distance across the wall from one corner of the room to another. The area of the wall is its length multiplied by its height.**

# Measuring areas

To figure out the area of a wall, you need to know both its length and its height. The length is the distance across the wall. The height is the distance from floor to ceiling. The area of a wall is the length times the height. If the wall were longer or higher, it would have more area.

## LENGTH, AREA, AND PERIMETER

A rectangle is a shape with four sides and four right angles. We can find the length of a rectangular field by measuring it in one direction. The area of the field is its length times its width. The perimeter of the field is the distance around the area. That is the length of all the edges added together.

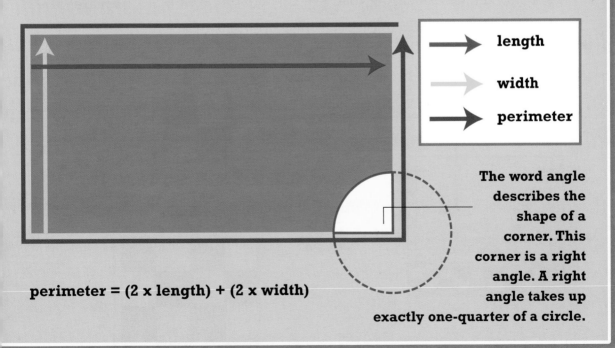

perimeter = (2 x length) + (2 x width)

**length**

**width**

**perimeter**

The word angle describes the shape of a corner. This corner is a right angle. A right angle takes up exactly one-quarter of a circle.

# MEASURING SQUARES

We measure lengths and distances with units such as inches, feet, and yards. Areas are measured in a different way. They have their own measurements called square units.

## Measuring floor area

Suppose the floor of a room is covered in square tiles. Each tile is a foot wide and a foot long. We could say the area of each tile measures 1 foot by 1 foot. There is a shorter way of saying that. We can say the area is 1 square foot. A square foot is a measurement of area.

▼ If the width and length of a square are both doubled, the square's area more than doubles.

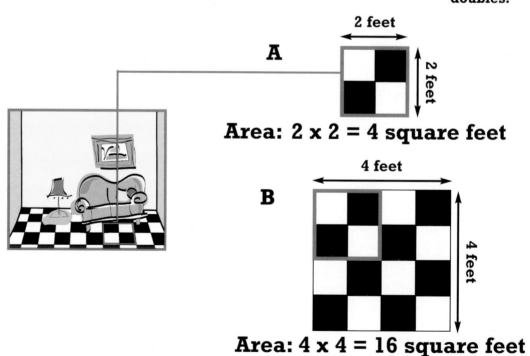

2 feet

A

2 feet

**Area: 2 x 2 = 4 square feet**

4 feet

B

4 feet

**Area: 4 x 4 = 16 square feet**

## MEASURE A FLOOR

Each tile is 1 foot times 1 foot. Suppose a part of the floor is five tiles wide and four tiles long. What is the area of that part of the floor?

The whole floor is eight tiles wide and eight tiles long. What is the area of the whole floor?

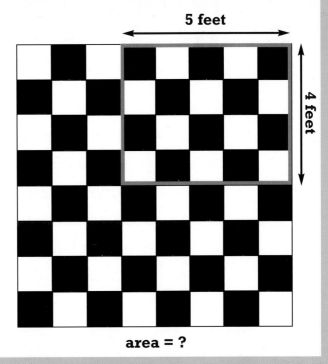

5 feet

4 feet

area = ?

+ − = x + − = x + − = x + − = x + − = + − = x + − = x + − =

## How length changes area

A small increase in length can make a big increase in area. Suppose a tiled floor is square. It is covered in tiles that are each 1 foot square. Imagine the floor measures two tiles long by two tiles wide (A, at left). Its area is 4 square feet ($2 \times 2 = 4$). Now suppose the floor measures four tiles long by four tiles wide (B, at left). That doubles the length of the floor in each direction. But the new area is four tiles by four tiles, or 16 square feet. So, doubling the length increases the area by four times.

> **FACT**
>
> A checkerboard has 64 squares. Each square measures 2 inches by 2 inches.

**WORD BANK**   *Square foot: an area that measures 1 foot times 1 foot*

# METRIC MEASUREMENTS

▶▶▶▶ **J**ust as we can use metric units, such as centimeters and meters, to measure length, we can also use metric units to measure area. Metric areas include square millimeters, square centimeters, square meters, and square kilometers.

Square kilometers would be used to measure the area of the whole city.

Square meters would be used to measure the area of a baseball field.

# Units are important

Square millimeters measure small things. You could use square centimeters to measure the area of a page in your reading book, for example, or the size of a playing card. Square meters could be used to measure the area of your school playground. People would use square kilometers to measure the area of a state or a country.

## ▶ METRIC AND IMPERIAL

It is possible to change imperial measurements of area to metric measurements of area.

Metric measurements of area can also be changed back into imperial measurements of area.

### IMPERIAL

1 square inch =
  6 $\frac{1}{2}$ square centimeters
1 square foot =
  930 square centimeters
1 square yard =
  $\frac{4}{5}$ square meter
1 square mile =
  2 $\frac{3}{5}$ square kilometers

### METRIC

1 square centimeter =
  $\frac{1}{6}$ square inch
1 square meter =
  10 $\frac{3}{4}$ square feet
1 square meter =
  1 $\frac{1}{5}$ square yards
1 square kilometer =
  $\frac{2}{5}$ square mile

**WORD BANK**   *Unit: a measurement of something*

# LARGE AND SMALL AREAS

▶▶▶ **S**quare feet and square meters are good for measuring the areas of floors. Smaller areas than that can be measured in square inches or square centimeters.

▶ **TRY THIS**

+ − = x + − = x + − = x +

## MEASURE AN AREA

> **Area of this hand**
> **= 6 square inches**
> **= *39 square centimeters***

**If a room = 10 feet x 15 feet**
What is its area in square feet?
*What is its area in square meters?*

**If a library book's cover**
**= 10 inches x 8 inches**
What is its area in square inches?
*What is its area in square centimeters?*

**Answers on page 31.**

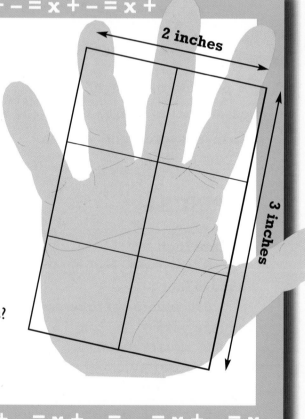

2 inches

3 inches

+ − = x + − = x + − = x + − = x + − = − = x + − = x

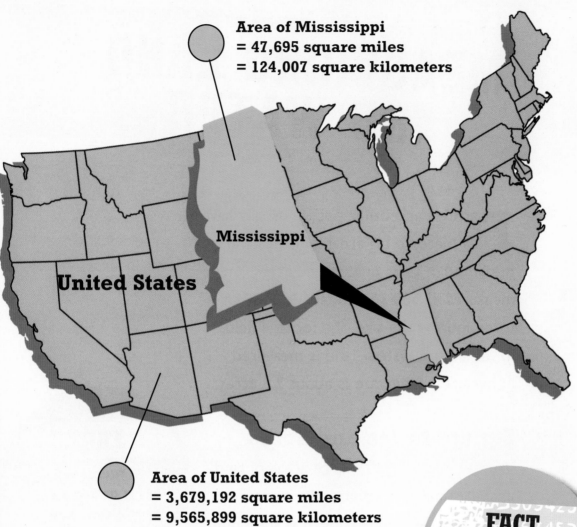

**Area of Mississippi**
**= 47,695 square miles**
**= 124,007 square kilometers**

Mississippi

United States

**Area of United States**
**= 3,679,192 square miles**
**= 9,565,899 square kilometers**

**FACT**

*Alaska is the biggest state. It covers an area 429 times as big as the smallest, Rhode Island.*

## Very big areas

Larger areas can be measured in square yards or square miles in the imperial system, or in square meters or square kilometers in the metric system. A square mile measures one mile long by one mile wide, so it is a huge area.

# MEASURING LAND AND WATER

**F**armers and other people usually have to measure big areas of land. Land is measured in large units called acres. An acre measures 43,560 square feet. It is about three-fourths the size of a football field. In the metric system, land is measured in hectares. A hectare is about 2.5 acres.

## Square miles and acres

We can measure very large areas of land in square miles. A square mile measures 1 mile long by 1 mile wide. It is the same size as 640 acres.

**FACT**

One square mile is as big as 640 acres, or almost 500 football fields!

▶ The area of a farmer's field could be as much as 30 or even 100 acres. Can you work out the area of the field marked on this photograph, in square feet?

# THE GREAT LAKES

Acres can be used to measure areas of water as well as land. The biggest areas of water in North America are the Great Lakes. Each lake covers a huge area that is the same size as millions of football fields!

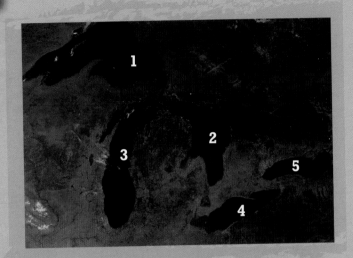

| Lake | Area (square miles) | How many football fields is that? |
| --- | --- | --- |
| 1 Superior | 31,700 | 15 million |
| 2 Huron | 23,000 | 11 million |
| 3 Michigan | 22,300 | 11 million |
| 4 Erie | 9,910 | 5 million |
| 5 Ontario | 7,550 | 4 million |

400 feet

900 feet

900 feet

400 feet

# MEASURING SIMPLE SHAPES

▶▶▶ **I**t is easy to figure out the area of a square. A square is a kind of rectangle. A square has four sides of equal length and four right angles. For any rectangle, the area is simply the length times the width. A rectangle is also a kind of parallelogram. A parallelogram is a shape with sides that are parallel. (Parallel lines are the same distance apart along their whole length.) A parallelogram's area is its length times its height.

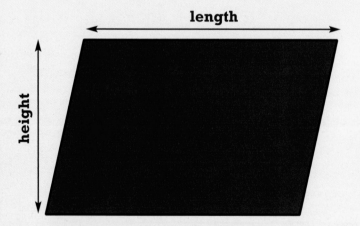

▲ Above is a parallelogram. The area of a parallelogram is its length times its height.

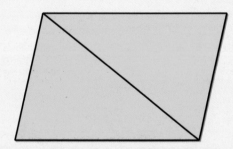

▲ Two matching triangles put together make a parallelogram.

4 square feet

Huge crowds gather for rock concerts and other special events. People can figure out the size of a crowd if they know how big an area the crowd fills. Say each person takes up roughly 4 square feet of ground, and the total area of the place is 8,000 square feet. Dividing the total area of the place by the area each person takes up tells how many people are in the crowd. In this case, 8,000 divided by 4 is 2,000 people.

## The area of a triangle

It is also easy to figure out the area of a triangle. If you take two identical triangles and put them together, you make a parallelogram. The area of each triangle is half the area of the parallelogram. The area of a parallelogram is its length times its height. The area of each triangle is equal to half of the parallelogram's area. So, the area of a triangle is half the length of its base times its height.

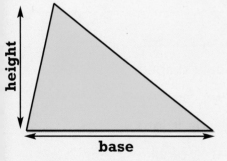

▲ The area of a triangle is half the length of its base times its height.

**WORD BANK** *Parallel lines: straight lines that are the same distance apart*

# MEASURING TOUGHER SHAPES

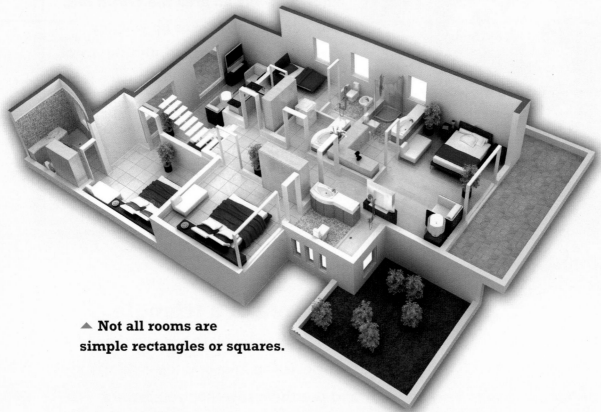

▲ **Not all rooms are simple rectangles or squares.**

**W**e often need to find the size of areas that are not simple shapes. Some oddly shaped areas look very hard to measure. But we can always take a complicated shape and divide it into simpler shapes. We can figure out the area of all the simple shapes. Then we add together these areas to find the area of the odd shape.

# Measuring an L-shaped room

Suppose, for instance, you need to figure out the area of an L-shaped room. You could split the L into three rectangles. The area of each rectangle is its length times its width. Find the area of each of the three rectangles. Add them all together to get the area of the room.

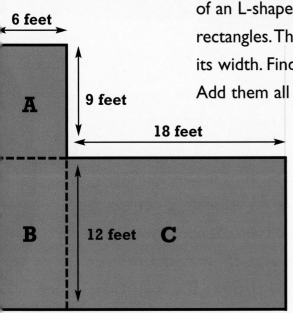

**A**: 6 feet x 9 feet = 54 square feet
**B**: 6 feet x 12 feet = 72 square feet
**C**: 12 feet x 18 feet = 216 square feet

**Area of the room =
54 + 72 + 216 = 342 square feet**

## TRY THIS

+ − = x + − = x + − = x + − = x + − = x + −

## WHAT SHAPES CAN YOU FIND?

Choose an unusually shaped room in your house and draw its outline, or perimeter, on a piece of paper. Can you divide its shape into simpler shapes? Can you figure out the area of the room?

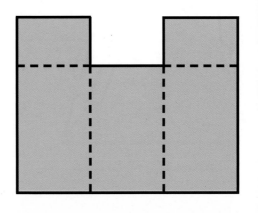

+ − = x + − = x + − = x + − = x + − = x + − = x + − = x + −

# MEASURING CIRCLES

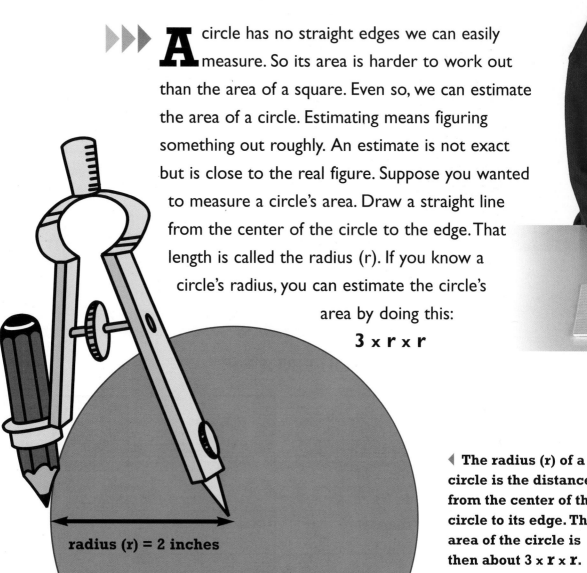

**A** circle has no straight edges we can easily measure. So its area is harder to work out than the area of a square. Even so, we can estimate the area of a circle. Estimating means figuring something out roughly. An estimate is not exact but is close to the real figure. Suppose you wanted to measure a circle's area. Draw a straight line from the center of the circle to the edge. That length is called the radius (r). If you know a circle's radius, you can estimate the circle's area by doing this:

**3 x r x r**

radius (r) = 2 inches

◀ The radius (r) of a circle is the distance from the center of the circle to its edge. The area of the circle is then about 3 x r x r.

**3 x r x r = estimated area of a circle**

+ – = x + – = x

## THE MAGIC NUMBER PI

To get the exact area of a circle, we use a special number called pi. This number is often written like this: π. Pi is the number 3.141. To figure out the exact area of a circle with a radius of 4 inches, do this (your answer should be in square inches):

**3.141 x r x r = area**

You will need to use a calculator!

+ – = x + – = x + – = x + – =

▲ Once you have figured out the radius of the circle, you can find out the circle's exact area using 3.141 x r x r.

**FACT**

A junior basketball has a radius of 4.35 inches (11 centimeters).

If you swap "r" for your circle's radius, the answer is the area of your circle. Imagine that the radius of your circle is 2 inches. Can you figure out the area? (A good estimate of its area is 3 x 2 x 2 = 12 square inches. The exact figure is 3.141 x 2 x 2 = 12.564 square inches.)

**WORD BANK**   *Pi: the number 3.141*

# AREAS OF CUBES AND SPHERES

▲ **A photograph of Earth taken from space. Earth's surface area is about 200 million square miles (510 million square kilometers).**

It is not only flat things that have an area. A tennis ball is a curved object called a sphere. The part of the sphere we can see is its outer surface. That surface has an area. We call it the surface area.

Our planet, Earth, is a bit like a gigantic tennis ball. We do not notice that Earth is round because it is so big, unless we see photographs of Earth taken

▲ The surface area of a tennis ball is about 25 square inches (160 square centimeters).

from space. Some parts of Earth are covered by fields, tennis courts, and parking lots.

## Curved, not flat

To us, these things look like flat areas. In fact, they sit on top of Earth's curved surface, so they are also slightly curved. Every field on Earth makes up a tiny part of its huge surface area.

▶ TRY THIS

+ – = x + – = x + – = x          – = – = x

### SURFACE AREA OF A CUBE

A cube has six identical faces. Each face is a square. The area of a square is its height times its width. So the surface area of a cube must be six times bigger. If the height of the cube is 2 inches, what is the cube's total surface area?

▶ If we flatten out a cube, we can see that it is made up of six identical faces. Each face is a square. So the area of the cube is 6 x height x width.

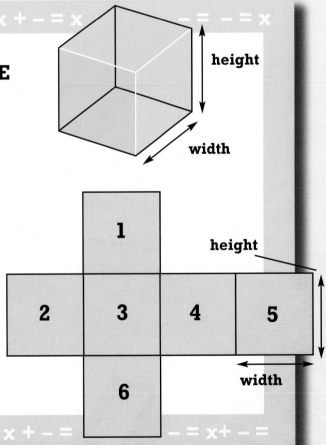

+ – = x + – = x + – = x + – = x + – =          – = x+ – =

# AREAS FOR PLANNING

**A**reas can be useful in everyday life. Farmers often need to know how much seed to plant in their fields. One way they can do this is to measure the area of each field. Then they know how much seed to buy and how much to plant so their crops grow evenly.

**FACT**

The construction site for a Dubai theme park is three times the area of Walt Disney World!

# AREAS AROUND YOUR HOME

Areas can be a big help at home. They can help you figure out how much icing to put on a birthday cake. If you are wrapping a present, you must know how much paper you need before you start. If you know the size, or area, of the present, that tells you how much wrapping paper you need.

▲ You need more paper to wrap bigger presents.

◀ When people are building a new highway, they need to know how much space, or area, it will take up so they get enough materials for the job. And there is no point in buying too many materials because they will never be used.

## Planning ahead

Area is also very useful for builders. If people are planning a new highway, they need to know how much space it will take up. They use maps and photographs to help them.

By figuring out the area of land they need, they can find out how much material they need to build the road. They can also figure out how much the highway will cost to build.

**WORD BANK**  *Map: a plan of some part of Earth*

# AREAS FROM ON HIGH

▶▶▶ **S**uppose people want to measure the area of a country. It is not an easy thing to do. First of all, a country is not a simple shape. It has lots of jagged bits around the edges. And even a small country takes up a huge area. It would be very hard to measure a country with a ruler!

## Aerial photographs

Larger areas are best measured from the sky, using a photograph of the ground taken from high up in an airplane. This kind of photograph has a name: it is called an aerial photograph.

On an aerial photograph, buildings, fields, and whole cities look like squares and other simple shapes. If we measure their areas on the photograph with a ruler, we can figure out their real areas by scaling up.

▶ **On an aerial photograph (like the one of Long Island, at right), we can figure out the size of a park by measuring it with a ruler on a map and scaling up.**

## SCALING UP

Suppose we have an aerial photograph of a park that we know the area of. We might measure the area of the park on the photograph.

Suppose we find that it takes up 1 square inch on the photograph. In real life, the park is 1 acre. So we know that 1 square inch on the photograph is the same as 1 acre of real land.

A different park on the photograph measures 12 square inches. Its real size must be 12 times 1 acre, or 12 acres:

$$12 \times 1 = 12 \text{ acres}$$

# LARGE AREAS ON EARTH

**P**hotographs taken from space satellites tell us a great deal about planet Earth. A satellite is a spacecraft without a crew that orbits (or moves around) Earth hundreds of miles above the ground.

The study of Earth is called geography. One of the things satellite photographs show is that seven-tenths of Earth is covered by water. Satellite photographs also show us the areas of the continents. They help us measure the area of

▼ This photograph, taken from a satellite, shows that much of Earth's surface is covered by water.

Satellite photographs have helped people see that Earth's forests are disappearing. People use satellite photographs to measure the area covered by forests each year. Each year, forested areas get smaller.

different states. They show how much of Earth's area is farmland and how much is covered by towns and cities.

## Changing Earth

If people take a satellite photograph from the same place every year, they can see how Earth is changing. Scientists are using satellite photographs to study global warming. That is the way Earth is slowly warming up because of things people do, such as burning coal and gas. Satellite photographs show the area of ice at the North Pole is slowly getting smaller. That suggests Earth is getting hotter. Studying areas is one way we can help save our planet.

**FACT**

From 2000 through 2010, an area of Brazil's forest the size of Georgia was destroyed.

**WORD BANK**    *Satellite: an uncrewed spacecraft*

# WHAT SIZE IS YOUR ROOM ?

## YOU WILL NEED

- **A large packet of paper (such as computer printer paper)**
- **A ruler**
- **A pencil**

 **WHAT TO DO**

**1.** First measure the area of one piece of paper. Use the ruler to measure its length in inches. Then measure its width in inches. Multiply the length of the paper by its width. Write down the result.

**2.** Take some more paper out of the packet. Now very carefully cover the floor of your room with pieces of paper.

**3.** When the floor is covered as completely as possible, count how many pieces of paper you have put down.

**4**. Multiply this number by the area of the first sheet of paper. The number you get is an estimate of the area of your floor in square inches.

**Can you figure out other ways to measure the area of your room?**

## This may help ...

Make sure the edges of the paper touch. But do not let the papers cover each other. Try to cover the floor completely so that all you can see is paper.

There will be parts of the floor that you cannot cover. Leave those areas.

# GLOSSARY

**area** The amount of space taken up by the surface of something.

**estimate** A rough measurement.

**geography** The study of Earth.

**length** The distance between two points, usually measured in a straight line.

**map** A plan of some part of Earth. A map is drawn as though from high up looking down.

**parallel lines** Straight lines that are always the same distance apart.

**parallelogram** A four-sided shape in which every side is parallel to the opposite side.

**perimeter** The distance around the edge of a shape.

**pi** A number used to figure out areas of circles. Pi has the value 3.141 and is often written as the symbol $\pi$.

**radius** The distance from the center of a circle to the edge.

**rectangle** A four-sided shape with right-angled corners.

**right angle** The angle made by two lines meeting at 90 degrees, such as at the corner of a square.

**satellite** An uncrewed spacecraft that can take photographs of Earth.

**scale up** To figure out how big something is from a map.

**square foot** A unit of area that measures 1 foot long by 1 foot wide.

**square inch** A unit of area that measures 1 inch long by 1 inch wide.

**square mile** A unit of area that measures 1 mile long by 1 mile wide.

**square unit** A measurement of area. Square feet and square inches are examples of square units.

**square yard** A unit of area that measures 1 yard long by 1 yard wide.

**surface area** The area that covers the surface of an object.

**unit** A measurement of something. Examples of units are inches and yards.

# FIND OUT MORE

## BOOKS

Marcie Aboff, *The Tallest Snowman.* Minneapolis, MN: Picture Window, 2008.

Brian Cleary, *How Long or How Wide?* Minneapolis, MN: Millbrook, 2007.

Jerry Pallotta, *Weights and Measures.* New York, NY: Scholastic, 2008.

Victoria Parker, *How Tall Is Tall: Comparing Structures.* Chicago, IL: Heinemann Library, 2011.

Henry Pluckrose, *What Size Is It?* North Mankato, MN: Sea to Sea Publications, 2007.

## WEBSITES

**Metric conversion chart**
Convert areas from imperial to metric and metric to imperial.
http://www.sciencemadesimple.com/area_conversion.php

**Johnnie's Math Page**
Measurement puzzles designed to increase your measuring ability.
http://jmathpage.com/JIMSMeasurementlengthmassvolume.html

**Interactive measurement games**
http://www.apples4theteacher.com/math.html
#measurementgames

**Publisher's note to educators and parents:** Our editors have carefully reviewed these websites to ensure that they are suitable for students. Many websites change frequently, however, and we cannot guarantee that a site's future contents will continue to meet our high standards of quality and educational value. Be advised that students should be closely supervised whenever they access the Internet.

*Answers to questions on page 10*
If a room is 10 feet x 15 feet, its area is 150 square feet, or 14 square meters.
If a library book's cover is 10 inches by 8 inches, its area is 80 square inches, or 520 square centimeters.

# INDEX